They Shall SPEAK With New Tongues

Ayodeji David Olusanmi

THEY SHALL SPEAK WITH NEW TONGUES
by Ayodeji David Olusanmi

Copyright ©2017 by Ayodeji David Olusanmi
ISBN: 978-1-64007-166-7
Contact Copyright Holder at
Ayodeji D. Olusanmi
Baruch Publishing
152 Oval Road North Dagenham,
Essex RM10 9EH
England

a.ilesanmi85@yahoo.co.uk

All Right Reserved. No part of this publication may be reproduced, stored in a retrieval system, or transmitted in any form or by any means without the express written consent of the copyright holder.

Unless otherwise noted, all Scripture quotations are taken from the King James Version of the Holy Bible, which is in the public domain.

Scripture noted AMP are taken from the Amplified Bible, Copyright ©1954, 1958, 1962, 1965, 1978 by The Lockman Foundation. All rights reserved.

Scriptures noted NLT are taken from the Holy Bible. New Living Translation copyright © 1996, 2004, 2007 by Tyndale House Foundation. All rights reserved.

APPRECIATION

We are to give honour to whom it is due. I would like to honour Dr Daniel K. Olukoya, the General Overseer of Mountain of Fire and Miracles Ministries Worldwide for all he has done and is doing for me. Daddy, your impact in my life cannot be quantified. My wife and I love you. I thank God for giving me a place to serve in MFM. It is an honour to partake of your grace, Sir.

I would also like to honour Rev & Rev (Mrs) Olusola Areogun, the General Overseer of Life Oasis International Church (The Dream Centre). Daddy, Mummy, my wife and I are grateful for the words you have sown in our lives over the years that we have followed your ministry. My wife and I appreciate the wisdom that comes to us from you anytime we are privileged to meet you. We treasure those moments from the core of our hearts.

I would, further, like to honour Pastor (Mrs) Tinu Olajide, Assistant Regional Overseer, Mountain of Fire and Miracle Ministries, Sweden & Finland; firstly, for your constant spiritual and moral input, and guidance into me and my wife's lives. And secondly, for taking time out to help edit, correct and proofread the manuscripts. Your input is highly appreciated.

Finally, I also honour those who have been a blessing to me over the years. God will reward your labour of love abundantly.

Amen!

DEDICATION

I DEDICATE THIS BOOK TO MY WIFE – MARGARET OLU-WASEUN OLUSANMI – WHO HAS BEEN A TREMENDOUS HELP IN MY LIFE AND MINISTRY. INDEED, A HELPER SUITABLE FOR ME!

CONTENT

INTRODUCTION 1

Chapter1:
DIVINE UTTERANCE BY THE SPIIT | 4

Chapter 2:
MUST I SPEAK IN TONGUES? | 9

Chapter 3:
BENEFITS OF SPEAKING IN TONGUES | 19

Chapter 4:
DIVERSE KINDS OF TONGUES
versus SPEAKING WITH NEW TONGUES | 47

Chapter 5:
PRACTICAL STEPS TO
RECEIVING THE HOLY SPIRIT | 61

Chapter 6:
A BETTER WAY TO PRAY | 68

INTRODUCTION

"Afterward he appeared unto the eleven as they sat at meat, and upbraided them with their unbelief and hardness of heart, because they believed not them which had seen him after he was risen. And he said unto them, Go ye into all the world, and preach the gospel to every creature. He that believeth and is baptized shall be saved; but he that believeth not shall be damned. And these signs shall follow them that believe; In my name shall they cast out devils; they shall speak with new tongues; They shall take up serpents; and if they drink any deadly thing, it shall not hurt them; they shall lay hands on the sick, and they shall recover" **Mark 16:14-18**

Jesus, whilst rounding up his earthly ministry, gave the Apostles a great task which is commonly called "The Great Commission". He moved on from that and said that there were some signs that would follow anyone who believes in Him. Apart from the fact that anyone who believes in Jesus would be saved and not be damned, there were other things that would begin to follow such people.

These were the signs Jesus said would follow such a person:

1. They will cast out devils (Demons or unclean spirit) in Jesus' name.
2. They will speak with new tongues (They will receive a prayer language)

3.	They will be able to take up serpents. (This is divine immunity against Satanic attacks, for we know that the devil is called serpent, that old dragon – Rev 20:2)
4.	Peradventure they drink any deadly thing, they will not be hurt. (This is also divine immunity).
5.	They will lay hands on the sick, and the sick person will recover. (This is a supernatural ability against sickness, to bring wholeness and wellness unto anyone sick).

Jesus said all these five major signs will characterize the believer. All he needs to do is believe! The signs Jesus talked about can be divided into two, namely, power against satanic works and power for a dynamic prayer life.

This book is about the power for a dynamic prayer life because the other signs might not be fully experienced if the prayer life of the believer is not sound and dynamic.

I will show you why you must speak in tongues and the benefits. I will also endeavour to clarify some of the major misconceptions about the subject of speaking in tongues.

I pray that the Holy Spirit will open the eyes of your understanding and that as you read, the spirit of wisdom and revelation in the knowledge of the Lord will come upon you. I pray that you will see beyond the letters, and the Lord will take you into the experience of what you are about to read.

They Shall Speak With New Tongues

CHAPTER ONE

DIVINE UTTERANCE BY THE SPIRIT

"And when the day of Pentecost was fully come, they were all with one accord in one place. And suddenly there came a sound from heaven as of a rushing mighty wind, and it filled all the house where they were sitting. And there appeared unto them cloven tongues like as of fire, and it sat upon each of them. And they were all filled with the Holy Ghost, and began to speak with other tongues, as the Spirit gave them utterance" **Act 2:1-4.**

The fulfilment of what Jesus said, began to manifest in the book of Acts of the Apostle, after having waited in obedience to Jesus' instruction. The Holy Spirit came and empowered them to begin to speak with tongues. You need to take a good note of this experience, *"And suddenly there came a sound from heaven as of a rushing mighty wind, and it filled all the house where they were sitting. And there appeared unto them cloven tongues like as of fire, and it sat upon each of them. And they were all filled with the Holy Ghost, and began to speak with other tongues, as the Spirit gave them utterance"*

Suddenly, things changed, there was a sound from heaven and there was impartation of the diverse spiritual gift. The people in the upper room were all filled with the Holy Ghost, and began to speak in other tongues, as the Spirit gave them utterance. Once they were filled with the Holy Spirit, something happened, they began to speak in other tongues, and they received a prayer language. They were speakng in languages that they hadn't learnt or knownnaturally. Divine ability was released to all of them to say things supernaturally. Later, I will expand on this experience that happened on the day of Pentecost because it has been misconstrued by many, both within and outside the church. I remember somebody asked me, why is it that no one understands the speaking in tongues some people are praying in these days? and made reference to the fact that the Pentecost experience was not like that, that there were people around, who understood what was being said.

In this chapter, what I want you to see is that, it was the Holy Spirit that gave them utterance. It was not a natural experience, it was supernatural. Whatever you can do by yourself without the Holy Spirit in the kingdom is natural, speaking in tongues is not one of such things. It is a supernatural experience that you must highly value. If you understand this, your relationship with the Holy Spirit will become stronger.

One major reason for this book is to clarify any misconceptions about speaking in tongues and bring understanding to some both within and outside the realm of the church. There are those who think they can copy or mimic the tongues – prayer language – of other people, this is unscriptural.

It is the Spirit that gives us the utterance, the Spirit gives us the words (syllables), we open our mouth as an act of faith and speak that which is bubbling up from within us – *"Out of his belly shall flow rivers of living water… this speak he of the Spirit…"* **John 7:38-39**.

Don't copy, let the Holy Spirit give you your own utterance. I don't know about you, but I like my things to be customised! That is exactly what he does, he customises the language for each person. By the grace of God, I have been praying for people to be filled with the Spirit for a while now and I have never heard two people speak the same language. The Holy Spirit has more than enough for us all.

You need to grasp what I am saying in this chapter so that you are not tossed to and fro with every wind of doctrine. The language that the Holy Spirit gives every believer is peculiar, very distinct and supernatural.

In the Bible, we see instances where people spoke in tongues. These happen immediately - and the Holy Spirit comes upon them or fills them up. We will look at some of these instances.

The first instance I want to elaborate is the experience at the house of Cornelius. By supernatural encounter, God spoke to both Peter and Cornelius in separate divine encounters by bringing the two together. This is the point where the agenda of God to graft in the Gentiles was unveiled.

Cornelius sent for Peter, as he arrived and began speaking, something happened, *"While Peter yet spake these words, the Holy Ghost fell on all them which heard the word. And they of the circumcision which believed were astonished, as many as came with Peter, because that on the Gentiles also was poured out the gift of the Holy Ghost. For they heard them speak with tongues, and magnify God. Then answered Peter, Can any man forbid water, that these should not be baptized, which have received the Holy Ghost as*

6

well as we?"* Acts 10:44-47. What happened was that the Holy Spirit fell on them that heard Peter. How did hey know the Holy Spirit came on them? The Bible says, *"… For they heard them speak with tongues, and magnify God…"* as soon as the Holy Spirit came on them, the household of Cornelius began to speak in tongues. This was supernatural; it was the same Upper room (Pentecost) experience because the people who witnessed it were also in the upper room.

The second instance is also in the book of Acts of the Apostle. Paul had arrived in Ephesus, he met some disciples, these were born again but not experiencing the fullness of God. He asked the one million dollar question – have you received the Holy Ghost since you believed? I am not sure why Paul asked, but I can guess he was led by the Spirit to ask. The answer was rather scary; they had not heard anything about the Holy Spirit. Paul introduced the Holy Spirit to them and laid his hands upon them, the Bible says, *"…the Holy Ghost came on them, and they spake with tongues….."* Acts 19:6. The Spirit gave them the ability, he enabled them to speak what wasn't possible in the natural standpoint. This is the ministry of the Spirit. I will talk more about this Acts 19:1-7 experience in chapter two.

I recently came across a video on the internet which proves the fact that speaking in tongues is divine in origin. It was a test conducted on some believers who speak in tongues. The test sought to affirm what the people claimed happens when they pray. They were asked to pray both in tongues and in their natural human language which was English. The test found that when these people prayed in English, the front lobe of the brain, which is responsible for lan guage is very active, but when they spoke in tongues, this front lobe was not active. It confirms that it was their spirit that was doing the praying.

CHAPTER TWO

MUST I SPEAK IN TONGUES?

"I thank my God, I speak with tongues more than ye all"
1Cor 14:18.

The question many times from both within and outside the Church is that must everyone speak in tongues? Or do I have to speak in tongues? The answer to both questions is very simple and straight forward. I think what many people do not understand is that in this kingdom, no one is forced to do anything. You have your choices to make and reap the consequences.
Asking if you must speak in tongues is like asking if you must drink water after eating. When some people eat, they drink water as they go, some drink after the meal, some perhaps drink before the meal and there might be some who don't drink after the meal at all.

What am I saying? Speaking in tongues is so important, it is like not taking water after or during a meal. Personally, I drink as I eat and then drink after I finish. I love to drink water, lots of it as it cleanses the system and makes you healthier. If you don't drink water during or after a meal, you will agree with me that you are missing out on a balanced diet or a complete diet. Asking such questions is a sign of inadequate Bible knowledge – lack of understanding of God's word. If having a drink during or after a meal is so vital, then speaking in tongues is also very vital. If it wasn't vital, Jesus wouldn't have said we shall speak with new tongues. He said it because he knows we would need it.

Jesus made a statement, he said, *"I have yet many things to say unto you, **but ye cannot bear them now**. Howbeit when he, the Spirit of truth, is come, he will guide you into all truth: for he shall not speak of himself; but whatsoever he shall hear, that shall he speak: and he will shew you things to come. He shall glorify me: for he shall receive of mine, and shall shew it unto you."* John 16:12-14. He said he had many things to discuss with the Apostles, but they couldn't and wouldn't comprehend because the Holy Spirit hadn't come, but when the Holy Spirit comes, He will give the capacity and ability to comprehend. He will boost the level of their understanding.

From my personal experience, I noticed that my understanding increases as I speak in tongues, especially when I need to make decisions. I just know what to do. I don't think that would happen if I wasn't baptised in the Holy Spirit with the evidence of speaking in tongues.

What I am driving at in this chapter, is that to be born again alone without the evidence of speaking in tongues is not sufficient; you are missing a divine blessing.

I also remember somebody asking if she would make it to heaven without speaking in tongues? Yes, you would! You may get there quicker though. You see, that you are not speaking in tongues doesn't mean you would not enjoy some kingdom benefits, but certainly, you won't experience the best of God. One divine provision for experiencing the best of God is by speaking in tongues.

THE ONE MILLION DOLLAR QUESTION

If the baptism in the Holy Spirit, with the evidence of speaking in tongues, is not important, Paul the Apostle wouldn't have attached serious importance to it. We know it was very important to Paul when he told the Church at Corinth, *"I thank my God, I speak with tongues more than ye all... and forbid not to speak with tongues."* 1 Cor. 14:18&39. This was a Church that spoke in tongues a lot, but not as much as Paul. This was something Paul did everywhere and every time. If he didn't speak in tongues a lot how would he have been able to speak in tongues more than a whole congregation? If this was Paul's lifestyle, I think it ought to be ours too.

We also know that speaking in tongues was important to Paul because we have a Bible record of what happened when he got to Ephesus. *"And it came to pass, that, while Apollos was at Corinth, Paul having passed through the upper coasts came to Ephesus: and finding certain disciples, He said unto them, Have ye received the Holy Ghost, since ye believed? And they said unto him, We have not so much as heard whether there be any Holy Ghost. And he said unto them, Unto what then were ye baptized? And they said, Unto John's baptism. Then said Paul, John verily baptized with the baptism of repentance, saying unto the people, that they should believe on him which should come after him, that is, on Christ Jesus. When they heard this, they were baptized in the name of the Lord Jesus. And when Paul had laid his hands upon them, the Holy Ghost came on them; and they spake with tongues, and prophesied. And all the men were about twelve."* Acts 19:1-7.

As soon as he came into Ephesus and met about twelve disciples, he asked them if they had received the Holy Ghost since they believed? This question was so direct and straightforward. We need to ask people that question if they had received the Holy Spirit. The response was shocking, *"... And they said unto him, We have not so much as heard whether there be any Holy Ghost"*. The next question Paul asked them sounded to me like, *"who led you to Christ and didn't bring you in on this major move of God?"*

Every minister of the gospel must learn from this, not to allow the new convert to miss out on this divine provision. You must be thorough with the souls that God allows to pass through your hand. If they must go through fasting, let them go through it, if they must finish Bible in a year don't slack on them, if they must go through deliverance, run them through it. Minister the Holy Spirit baptism to them until everyone is speaking with tongues. What I do in our Church is whenever I call for those who are yet to receive the baptism of the Holy Spirit with evidence of speaking in tongues, after teaching them what to expect and what to do. If these instructions are obeyed, God has always honoured His word with signs following.

If another person is now doing what you should have done for your converts, this probably means you have not been thorough with your assignment.

Did you also notice that these disciples had a level of revelation, but not in the full measure? They knew about John's baptism, which was repentance but had never heard about the Holy Spirit. Those who ask if it is necessary for them to speak in tongues most often are like these Ephesians' disciples, who have a level of understanding, but perhaps not deep enough to receive what God is doing next.

I need you to see the seriousness Paul attached to the baptism of the Holy Ghost with the evidence of speaking in tongues. Paul wondered how they could be effective in their ministry without this baptism. Did you notice that Paul ensured they were filled with the Holy Spirit before he left them? That is how important the baptism, in the Holy Spirit with the evidence of speaking in tongues, is.

YOU CAN BE BORN AGAIN AND NOT SPEAK IN TONGUES

Speaking in tongues and the salvation experience is different from each other, though some people experience both at the same time depending on the circumstances surrounding their salvation. All you need to do to be saved is, *"But what saith it? The word is nigh thee, even in thy mouth, and in thy heart: that is, the word of faith, which we preach; That if thou shalt confess with thy mouth the Lord Jesus, and shalt believe in thine heart that God hath raised him from the dead, thou shalt be saved. For with the heart man believeth unto righteousness; and with the mouth confession is made unto salvation"* Rom 10:8-10. Once you call on him and believe with your heart, you are born again according to the Bible.

Did you notice that this says nothing about speaking in any tongues, if this is all you get, you will make it to heaven. But we are not just trying to make it to heaven; we want to enjoy the best of God.

DISTINCTION: SALVATION & HOLY SPIRIT BAPTISM

Here, we shall see instances where individuals either got saved and baptised in the Holy Spirit with evidence of speaking in tongues at the same time, or got saved alone.

1.   The Ethiopian eunuch – Acts 8:27-38 (Salvation Only)

"And he arose and went: and, behold, a man of Ethiopia, an eunuch of great authority under Candace queen of the Ethiopians, who had the charge of all her treasure, and had come to Jerusalem for to worship, Was returning, and sitting in his chariot read Esaias the prophet. Then the Spirit said unto Philip, Go near, and join thyself to this chariot. And Philip ran thither to him, and heard him read the prophet Esaias, and said, Understandest thou what thou readest? And he said, How can I, except some man should guide me? And he desired Philip that he would come up and sit with him. The place of the scripture which he read was this, He was led as a sheep to the slaughter; and like a lamb dumb before his shearer, so opened he not his mouth: In his humiliation his judgment was taken away: and who shall declare his generation?, for his life is taken from the earth. And the eunuch answered Philip, and said, I pray thee, of whom speaketh the prophet this?, of himself, or of some other man? Then Philip opened his mouth, and began at the same scripture, and preached unto him Jesus. And as they went on their way, they came unto a certain water: and the eunuch said, See, here is water; what doth hinder me to be baptized? And Philip said, If thou believest with all thine heart, thou mayest. And he answered and said, I believe that Jesus Christ is the Son of God. And

he commanded the chariot to stand still: and they went down both into the water, both Philip and the eunuch; and he baptized him"

This was a man of Ethiopia, a ready harvest, waiting to be brought into the kingdom. Philip met him, elaborated to him the same scripture he met him reading and baptised him with water. This man was saved under the ministry of Philip but wasn't baptised in the Holy Spirit with the evidence of speaking in tongues. The Bible says, *"And when they were come up out of the water, the Spirit of the Lord caught away Philip, that the eunuch saw him no more: and he went on his way rejoicing."* Acts 8:39.

2.   The people of Samaria. (Acts 8:5-17)

In this case, they got saved under the ministry of Philip but the apostle came later from Jerusalem to pray for them to receive the Holy Spirit. *"Then Philip went down to the city of Samaria, and preached Christ unto them. And the people with one accord gave heed unto those things which Philip spake, hearing and seeing the miracles which he did. For unclean spirits, crying with loud voice, came out of many that were possessed with them: and many taken with palsies, and that were lame, were healed. And there was great joy in that city. But there was a certain man, called Simon, which beforetime in the same city used sorcery, and bewitched the people of Samaria, giving out that himself was some great one: To whom they all gave heed, from the least to the greatest, saying, This man is the great power of God. And to him they had regard, because that of long time he had bewitched them with sorceries. But when they believed Philip preaching the things concerning the kingdom* of God, and the name of Jesus Christ, they were baptized, both men and women. Then Simon himself believed also: and when he was baptized, he continued with Philip, and wondered, beholding the miracles and signs which were done.

Up until this point, they were born again, but they weren't filled or baptised in the Holy Spirit with evidence of speaking in tongues. Somehow, word got around and the apostles at Jerusalem heard that Samaria had received the gospel, they sent to them Peter and John. When these two arrived, what didn't happen before, began to happen, Bible says, *"...Now when the apostles which were at Jerusalem heard that Samaria had received the word of God, they sent unto them Peter and John: Who, when they were come down, prayed for them, that they might receive the Holy Ghost: (FOR AS YET HE WAS FALLEN UPON NONE OF THEM: ONLY THEY WERE BAPTIZED IN THE NAME OF THE LORD JESUS.)Then laid they their hands on them, and they received the Holy Ghost"* Though this didn't say for certain that they spoke in tongues, but in many ways, going by the pattern of the New Testament we can conclude that after hands were laid on them and the Holy Spirit fell upon them, they would have spoken in tongues. This statement *"... (FOR AS YET HE WAS FALLEN UPON NONE OF THEM: ONLY THEY WERE BAPTIZED IN THE NAME OF THE LORD JESUS.)..."* put a clear distinction between the salvation and Holy Spirit baptism.

3.   *Cornelius Household (Acts 10)*

In this scenario, the two experiences – Salvation and Holy Spirit baptism with the evidence of speaking in tongues, I would say happened together. No altar call had been made yet, but mere hearing what Peter was saying, the Holy Spirit fell on them. *"While Peter yet spake these words, the Holy Ghost fell on all them which heard the word. And they of the circumcision which believed were astonished, as many as came with Peter, because that on the Gentiles also was poured out the gift of the Holy Ghost. For they heard them speak with tongues, and magnify God. Then answered Peter, Can any man forbid water, that these should not be baptized, which have received the Holy Ghost as well as we?" v44-47.* After this supernatural experience, Peter had them baptised in water, *"And he commanded them to be baptized in the name of the Lord." V48.*

It will be good to know that Cornelius was a good man; he gave alms every time, but was not born again, though It was said that he was, *"A devout man, and one that feared God with all his house, which gave much alms to the people, and prayed to God always"v2.* In my estimation, I would consider Cornelius and his household as individuals not far from the kingdom, who were ripe for harvest.

4.   The Disciples at Ephesus (Acts 19:1-7)

"And it came to pass, that, while Apollos was at Corinth, Paul having passed through the upper coasts came to Ephesus: and finding certain disciples, He said unto them, Have ye received the Holy Ghost since ye believed? And they said unto him, We have not so much as heard whether there be any Holy Ghost. And he said unto them, Unto what then were ye baptized? And they said, Unto John's baptism. Then said Paul, John verily baptized with the baptism of repentance, saying unto the people, that they should believe on

him which should come after him, that is, on Christ Jesus. When they heard this, they were baptized in the name of the Lord Jesus. And when Paul had laid his hands upon them, the Holy Ghost came on them; and they spake with tongues, and prophesied. And all the men were about twelve."

It is logical to come to the conclusion that these disciples had been born again for a while, but had neither heard nor received the baptism in the Holy Spirit. They got saved under the ministry of John the Baptist, which Paul confirmed as a baptism of repentance. Paul later, *"laid his hands upon them, the Holy Ghost came on them; and they spake with tongues, and prophesied. And all the men were about twelve."*

This is another event that confirms that the salvation experience is different from the Holy Spirit baptism with evidence of speaking in tongues. When you are born again, you are born of the Spirit, but to be filled with the Holy Spirit is to be baptised in the Holy Spirit with the evidence of speaking in tongues. (See John 3:5-6, 8. Acts 2:4 & Eph 5:18).

CHAPTER THREE

BENEFITS OF SPEAKING IN TONGUES

"I thank my God, I speak with tongues more than ye all" 1 Cor. 14:18.

Jesus said these signs shall follow them who believes in him –

1.   They shall cast out demons in His name.
2.   They shall speak with new tongues.
3.   They will take up serpents, and if they drink any deadly thing, it shall not hurt them.
4.   They will lay hands on the sick, and they shall recover.

We see these in Mark 16:17-18. All of these signs are significant in themselves because what was not happening before will suddenly begin to happen because you believe in Jesus.

We also saw earlier that Paul gave prominence to speaking in tongues. He said he spoke in tongues more than the Corinthian Church, he also said that they should not forbid anyone from speaking in tongues and finally, he asked the disciples at Ephesus if they had received the baptism with the evidence of speaking in tongues. If speaking in tongues has no benefits, I believe Jesus wouldn't say we will speak in tongues and Paul would not go about it the way he did. No matter how little the benefit may seem, I don't want to miss out on anything God has in store for me. I will elaborate in this chapter some benefits of speaking in tongues.

BENEFITS OF SPEAKING IN TONGUES:

It Will Help You Engage Your Spirit Man:

Paul said, *"For if I pray in an unknown tongue, my spirit prayeth, but my understanding is unfruitful"* 1Cor 14:14. When you speak in tongues, it is your spirit that is doing the prayer and not your mind. I mentioned earlier in chapter one about the test that was conducted which confirmed that it is the spirit that is doing the prayer. There was a man I pastored, who came and told me all of his problems. He has been born again for a long time, but not an active Christian, not engaged in kingdom pursuits. He is what you could refer to as a nominal Christian – he had the name, but no life. What I did, was to include him in the prayer programmes of the Church so that he can engage his spirit man. I gave him the prayer points to use in leading the Church to pray. One of his problems was bad dreams, after he engaged his spirit by praying fervently very well, there was a change in his dream life. All the oppressive dreams and afflictions reduced.

Man is a tripartite being; he is a spirit that has a soul which lives in a body. Paul said, "And the very God of peace sanctify you wholly; and I pray God your whole spirit and soul and body be preserved blameless unto the coming of our Lord Jesus Christ" 1Thess 5:23. Paul highlighted the distinction in the make up of man. With your spirit, you contact the spirit realm, with your soul, you contact the soulish realm and with your body, you make contact with the physical realm. The spirit is God conscious, the soul is self-conscious (this is the heart of emotions from where one's desires and needs stem from). The body is world conscious. One's body relates to the world through the five senses of touch, taste, smell, sight and hearing.

If you understand this, you will pay more attention to your spirit, and pray more in tongues. Jesus said that God is a spirit and those who will worship Him must do so in *spirit* and in truth. That, automatically, tells you that without the involvement of your spirit, your worship will be limited. Paul prayed for the Ephesian saints, *"For this cause I bow my knees unto the Father of our Lord Jesus Christ, Of whom the whole family in heaven and earth is named, That he would grant you, according to the riches of his glory, to be strengthened with might by his Spirit in the inner man"* Eph 3:14-16. He said that the Holy Spirit will strengthen not their soul, nor their bodies, but their spirit (inner) man, which was the real deal.

If you are not engaging your spirit man to do spiritual things such as speaking in tongues, what will happen is that your spirit will be dull, it will not be in a place to help you. Solomon said, *"The spirit of man is the candle of the Lord, searching all the inward parts of the belly."* Prov 20:27. *"The spirit of a man will sustain his infirmity; but a wounded spirit who can bear"* Prov 18:14.

Let's see a few things your spirit will do for you –

A. Your spirit is the candle of the Lord. What is the job of a candle? Jesus gave the answer to this, *"Neither do men light a candle, and put it under a bushel, but on a candlestick; and it giveth light unto all that are in the house."* Mat 5:15. Did you notice the phrase, *"it giveth light unto all that are in the house"*? That is if your spirit man is in the place it should be, you will be able to give light to all that are in your house. This means you will be in a position to help people in your circle of influence. You will be able to receive divine instructions and direction that will be a great blessing to the people. As a father, you will be able to help both your nuclear and extended family. As a boss at work, if your spirit is well lit, you will be able to help that organisation because they are the ones in your house so to speak. Apostle Paul had enough light in his spirit man to warn the captain of the ship he was aboard going to Italy, he told them, *"Sirs, I perceive that this voyage will be with hurt and much damage, not only of the lading and ship, but also of our lives. Nevertheless the centurion believed the master and the owner of the ship, more than those things which were spoken by Paul."* Acts 27:10-11. The captain didn't listen to Paul because he probably thought why should he listen to a novice. You may be a novice in the flesh, but not in the spirit. The Holy Spirit gives your spirit light as you meditate on the word and pray in tongues. To show that what Paul perceived was right, see what the Bible says, "**But not long after there arose against it a tempestuous wind, called Euroclydon.** *And when the ship was caught, and could not bear up into the wind, we let her drive. And running under a certain island which is called Clauda, we had much work to come by the boat: Which when they had taken up, they used helps, undergirding the ship; and, fearing lest they should fall into the quicksands, strake sail, and so were driven. And we being exceedingly tossed with a tempest, the next day they lightened the ship; And the third day we cast out with our own hands the tackling of the ship. And when neither sun nor stars in many days appeared, and no small tempest lay on us, all hope that we should be saved was then taken away. But after long abstinence Paul stood forth in the midst of them, and said, Sirs, ye should have hear kened* *unto me, and not have loosed from Crete, and* **to have gained this harm and loss**" Acts 27:14-21. They almost died and had to go through unnecessary 14 days of fasting, all because they disobeyed the light - direction – Paul perceived in his spirit. Whenever you disobey the direction from the Holy Spirit to your spirit man, you may pay dearly for it. It took the mercy of God for them to survive. Daddy Areogun usually say, "It is better to err on the side of caution than on the side of action"

What you should learn very well is how to use your spirit to search for things so that you are not in darkness. There are decisions you will have to make that you can't afford to be wrong in, because of the effect it might have on you. For example, if you will marry the right person, you have to engage the Holy Spirit, expect him to guide and lead you. You see, the fact that a brother or sister looks good, beautiful and harmless on the outside it does not necessarily mean s/he is genuine on the inside. Learn to ask the Holy Spirit to X-ray people for you. There are wolves in sheep's clothing!

B. Your spirit will sustain your infirmity. The book of Jude said, *"... building up yourselves.... (By) praying in the Holy Ghost"* When you possess a strong spirit man, your spirit will be in a position to help you and also fight away any infirmity that might come your way. The Amplified version, Classic Edition of Prov. 18:4 says, *"The strong spirit of a man sustains him in bodily pain or trouble, but a weak and broken spirit who can raise up or bear?"* Do you notice it says the strong spirit of a man? That was why Paul prayed for the Church at Ephesus to be strengthened with might in the inner man.

C. Your spirit will receive inspiration and understanding. The book of Job says, *"But there is a spirit in man: and the inspiration of the Almighty giveth them understanding."* Job 32:8. If your spirit has been developing over a period of time, it will be a source of inspiration for you.

Speaking In Tongues Will Edify – Build – You:

The Amplified version of Jude 20 says, "But ye, beloved, building up yourselves on your most holy faith, praying in the Holy Ghost," The Amplified Version render it like this, "But you, beloved, build yourselves up on [the foundation of] your most holy faith [continually progress, rise like an edifice higher and higher], pray in the Holy Spirit," I remember when I taught on this subject in our Church and I showed two pictures, one of a bungalow and the other of a high rise tower building. I told the Church to choose which one they wanted to be like, you know everyone chose the high rise building. At that point, I dropped the bombshell, "If you are not praying in tongues, you are like a bungalow"

The only way to rise like an edifice - higher and higher is by constantly praying in tongues.

Speaking In Tongues Will Help Your Faith:

If you speak a lot in tongues, one thing you will observe is that your faith is stimulated. Jude 20, which we already looked at says, "But ye, beloved, building up yourselves on your most holy faith, praying in the Holy Ghost". Speaking in tongues will not give or supply you faith because the Bible says, "Faith cometh by hearing, and hearing by the word of God" Rom 10:17. Every believer has a measure of faith, what is now required is to build it up, make it stronger by praying in tongues. When this is done, you will see that you are able to believe God for things that perhaps you wouldn't have before. I have, personally, noticed that there were things I couldn't do but could do later after I have prayed much in the spirit. I perceive a mantle of boldness coming upon my spirit after spending time in prayer. If you don't pray much, you may not have the audacity to do some things that you ought to do. The reason, many waiver, is due to lack of faith and a strong prayer life. I remember when the Lord spoke to my heart that my wedding was to be done within 52days. I had been reading a book – *The Apprentice Leader* -, and the author – Andrew Fox - spoke about how Nehemiah finished the wall in 52 days and the word of the Lord came to me from there. Faith came to me, I calculated the dates on the spot and I called my fiancée – Margaret - who is now my wife. I told her that the Lord just spoke to me and the dates I have chosen. She agreed and the fight of faith started. We met with some obstacles, but praying much in tongues helped to sustain the fire of the faith that came to me.

Speaking In Tongues Help You To Bless Accurately:

Paul said, *"Else when thou shalt bless with the spirit…"* 1Cor 14:16. He said it was possible to bless with the spirit. Blessing in your understanding is good, but a blessing in tongues is far greater, especially when you perceive that the Holy Spirit is leading you in this direction. You must understand that God places a high value on blessing, when He was going to bless the children of Israel, He gave words that were to be spoken and Aaron had to say it verbatim. Let's look at it, *"And the LORD spake unto Moses, saying Speak unto Aaron and unto his sons, saying, On this wise ye shall bless the children of Israel, saying unto them, The LORD bless thee, and keep thee: The LORD make his face shine upon thee, and be gracious unto thee: The LORD lift up his countenance upon thee, and give thee peace. And they shall put my name upon the children of Israel, and I will bless them"* Num 6:22-27. Did you notice the phrase, *"On this wise ye shall bless the children of Israel, saying unto them…"* He had to bless them in a particular way by saying specific words, not just anything that he likes. Did you also notice that the blessing was in seven categories? Let us break it down –

1. The Lord bless thee.

2. The Lord keep thee.

3. The Lord makes his face shine upon thee.

4. The Lord is gracious on to thee.

5. The Lord lift up his countenance upon thee.

6. The Lord give you peace.

7. They shall put the Lord's name on the children of Israel (Divine support, intervention, mark of exemption from any form of evil and mark of favour to attract every good thing).

These were the words Aaron had to proclaim over them. No matter your challenges, you were covered and have your miracles once the blessings were said over you. I am fully persuaded that there is a depth of blessing we are able to enter into, by speaking in tongues, that otherwise wouldn't have been possible.

Speaking In Tongues Provides The Best Way To Give Thanks:

Paul, is bringing revelation into what goes on when we pray in tongues, says, *"For if I pray in an unknown tongue, my spirit prayeth, but my understanding is unfruitful. What is it then? I will pray with the spirit, and I will pray with the understanding also: I will sing with the spirit, and I will sing with the understanding also. Else when thou shalt bless with the spirit, how shall he that occupieth the room of the unlearned say Amen at thy giving of thanks, seeing he understandeth not what thou sayest? For thou verily givest thanks well, but the other is not edified"* 1Cor 14:14-17.

Praying or speaking in tongues enables us to give thanks and Paul said when we do it like that, we do it well. Do you understand that, we are not just doing a good job, but a great job because he said, *"For thou verily givest thanks well…"* The Greek word translated givest thanks well is KALOS, which means to do something finely, beautifully, excellently, honourably, nobly, commendably, rightly well, so that there will be no room for blame. When we speak in tongues, amongst other things happening is that we are giving thanks in the best way and Paul says when that is done there will be no room for blame.

Speaking In Tongues Enable A Believer To Magnify God.

We will consider the incident that took place in the house of Cornelius. We know they received the Holy Spirit with the evidence of speaking in tongues, but something also happened whilst they spoke in tongues. Bible says, *"While Peter yet spake these words, the Holy Ghost fell on all them which heard the word. And they of the circumcision which believed were astonished, as many as came with Peter, because that on the Gentiles also was poured out the gift of the Holy Ghost. For they heard them speak with tongues, and magnify God. Then answered Peter, Can any man forbid water, that these should not be baptized, which have received the Holy Ghost as well as we?"* Acts 10:44-47. The people were heard speaking in tongues and also magnifying God. The Amplified version reads, *"For they heard them talking in [unknown] tongues (languages) and exalting and magnifying and praising God."* As they prayed in tongues, they magnified God, and God got bigger in their eyes. They came into the consciousness of his greatness. I believe what happens is that, God gets bigger in our own eyes and our problems get smaller and smaller until victory comes. I recently went through a court case for an offence which I knew nothing about. The case went from the Magistrate to Crown Court. During this period, I prayed both in my understanding and in tongues, I realized that I was more conscious of the power of God and it settled within me that the case was going to be thrown out of court. Though I had people praying with and for me, my spiritual parents also gave me a word of prophecy. I never said a word to our congregation. I led the Church as if nothing was happening. There were days I would attend court in the morning and preach in our revival service in the evening. I remember the day of the trial was on a Monday, the previous day was Sunday, and we had an unusual move of God in Church. On Monday, the trial day, the case was adjourned and later thrown out of court. I believe one of the reasons I was able to go through it all, was because I prayed much in the spirit and God was magnified to me. I remember that whenever I went to the court for the case, I would usually pray in the spirit quietly until I am required to speak. There is a scripture that says, *"Thou wilt keep him in perfect peace, whose mind is stayed on thee: because he trusteth in thee. Trust ye in the LORD for ever: for in the LORD JEHOVAH is everlasting strength"* Is 26:3-4. This scripture is simply saying that as you focus on the Lord (One of the easiest ways to focus on the Lord is by speaking in tongues), God will be magnified to you, which will produce peace because in the LORD JEHOVAH is everlasting strength.

Speaking In Tongues Helps You Talk To God Directly:

Paul wrote to the Corinthian Church, *"For he that speaketh in an unknown tongue speaketh not unto men, but unto God: for no man understandeth him; howbeit in the spirit he speaketh mysteries...For if I pray in an unknown tongue, my spirit prayeth, but my understanding is unfruitful."* 1Cor 14:2 &14. When you pray in tongues, your natural mind has nothing to do with it, that was why Paul said, *"For if I pray in an unknown tongue, my spirit prayeth, but my understanding is unfruitful."* It is your spirit that is doing the praying as enabled by the Holy Spirit. The Amplified version is more explanatory, *"For if I pray in a tongue, my spirit prays, but my mind is unproductive [because it does not understand what my spirit is praying]."* By this, you are able to communicate directly. This is a great benefit because it gives the believer a direct line as it were to God, no one understands what is being spoken. This will allow you to get very private and intimate with God. Whenever I need to talk to my wife and I don't want any other person to participate, I speak our native language, of course, if you are not from there you won't understand anything we are saying.

Do you know we can cut the devil off by speaking in tongues? I remember a story I heard about a man whose wife was involved in an accident. He said he had difficulty believing God for the wife's healing because what happens was that as soon as he finishes praying, doubt will flood his mind. So, he changed tactics and began praying in the spirit, all of a sudden, he had a vision where he saw two demons sitting on his shoulders and whispering to each other, trying to figure out what kind of language he was speaking. After a while, he said the demons said to each other that they were feeling the heat and had to disappear. The devil does not understand us when we pray in tongues. The Amplified says, *"For one who speaks in an unknown tongue does not speak to people but to God; for no one understands him or catches his meaning, but by the Spirit he speaks mysteries [secret truths, hidden things]."* TLB says, *"But if your gift is that of being able to "speak in tongues," that is, to speak in languages you haven't learned, you will be talking to God but not to others, since they won't be able to understand you. You will be speaking by the power of the Spirit, but it will all be a secret"*. We speak divine secrets, truths and hidden things.

One of the challenges I have encountered in praying for people to receive the baptism in the Holy Ghost with the evidence of speaking in tongues is when they say to me, *"Why should I speak a language I don't understand"* or *"How am I certain that I am speaking the correct language"*. My answer is usually WE WALK BY FAITH AND NOT BY SIGHT. Paul said it is a language no one understands and it is a means to directly pray to God because my spirit is the one praying. I think that's a good bargain – being able to pray directly to God. The next benefit of praying in tongues which is closely related to this is that you will be able to pray more accurately or pray the will of God.

Speaking In Tongue Will Help You Pray Accurately Or Pray The Will Of God:

BENEFITS OF SPEAKING IN TONGUES

One thing many do not know is that you could pray and not get results because you prayed amiss. James said in his writing that, "…. *ye have not, because ye ask not. Ye ask, and receive not, because ye ask amiss…*" James 4:2-3. These were people doing a lot of asking but weren't receiving because they miss it. This is what makes speaking in tongues special to me because of what I am able to achieve. What is the essence of praying if I am going to pray amiss, and why won't I take advantage of a means that I know can never go wrong? Paul outlined our ordeal when it comes to prayer, he said, "*Likewise the Spirit also helpeth our infirmities: for we know not what we should pray for as we ought: but the Spirit himself maketh intercession for us with groanings which cannot be uttered. And he that searcheth the hearts knoweth what is the mind of the Spirit, because he maketh intercession for the saints according to the will of God. And we know that all things work together for good to them that love God, to them who are the called according to his purpose*" Rom 8:26-28.

Paul said the Holy Spirit helps our infirmities. The Greek word for infirmities is ASTHENEIA which means weakness. Paul is saying that there is a weakness we all have, when it comes to prayer, which only the Holy Spirit can deliver us from. This is the weakness - for we know not what we should pray for as we ought. The Amplified says, "*In the same way the Spirit [comes to us and] helps us in our weakness.* **We do not know what prayer to offer or how to offer it as we should**, *but the Spirit Himself [knows our need and at the right time] intercedes on our behalf with sighs and groanings too deep for words.*" The two weaknesses we have in prayer are as follows:

1.   We do not know what prayer to offer.
2.   We do not know how to offer it the right way. This is talking about the depth that is needed to go which is often unknown to us without the Holy Spirit

Seeing these weaknesses, the Holy Spirit comes to our aid. KJV says, "but the Spirit himself maketh intercession for us with groanings which cannot be uttered" AMP version, *"but the Spirit Himself [knows our need and at the right time] intercedes on our behalf with sighs and groanings too deep for words."* So, the question is, how does the Holy Spirit come to our rescue to intercede on our behalf with sighs and groanings too deep for words? He does this when we pray in the Holy Ghost. Praying in the Holy Ghost is also praying/speaking in tongues. Now, let's move further, what exactly does the Holy Spirit do, in bringing about accuracy when he helps us in prayer? Paul gave the answer by the Spirit; he said, *"And he that searcheth the hearts knoweth what is the mind of the Spirit, because he maketh intercession for the saints according to the will of God."* We can conclude that the Holy Spirit does two things:

1.   He *searches*..... He searches to know what is needed to be done.
2.   After searching..... he then *maketh intercession for you and I according to the will of God*. That is why you can never go wrong whilst speaking in tongues. Your natural ability can't do what searching the Spirit has the ability to do, so you can't get the results the Holy Spirit will get. It is wisdom to allow the master to do his job.

You will be limited, inaccurate and miss the will of God for your life if you do not pray in tongues. Let us look at what happens when we allow the Spirit to make inter- cession for us according to God's will. The Bible says, *"And we know that all things work together for good to them that love God, to them who are the called according to his purpose."* All things will not be good, but they will work together for good. Daddy Areogun said if it is not God sent, it will be God used. This implies that if God didn't organise that situation for you, he is able to use it for his glory.

All things will work together for good, for two categories of people - not everyone, but for those –

1. Who loves God.
2. Who are called according to his purpose.

You can't claim anything if you don't fall into the two categories.

Speaking In Tongues Helps You Operate In The Gifts Of The Spirit:

Speaking in tongues in itself is supernatural; it is safe to conclude that the more you engage in it the more you will move in the gifts of the Spirit. That means speaking in tongues is the doorway to the supernatural. Paul said, *"I would that ye all spake with tongues but rather that ye prophesied: for greater is he that prophesieth than he that speaketh with tongues, except he interpret, that the church may receive edifying... Wherefore let him that speaketh in an unknown tongue pray that he may interpret."* 1 Cor. 14:5&13. By Paul's writing, it's evident that speaking in tongues plus interpretation equals prophecy. Because, he said, *"for greater is he that prophesieth than he that speaketh with tongues, except he interpret,"* When you interpret what you said in tongues it is called prophecy. Paul said prophecy is for, "...*edification, and exhortation, and comfort.*" 1Cor 14:3.

To further understand the benefit of speaking in tongues as a doorway to flowing in other gifts of the Holy Spirit, I will outline the nine gifts –

1. The gift of word of wisdom.
2. The gift of word of knowledge.
3. The gift of faith.
4. The gifts of healing.
5. The gift of working of miracles.
6. The gift of prophecy.
7. The gift of discerning of spirits
8. The gift of diverse – different - kinds of tongues.
9. The gift of interpretation of tongues.

Bible teachers and commentators have divided these gifts into three groups for the purpose of easy reference. The division will help us understand these gifts more perfectly.

Power Gifts

1. Faith.
2. Gifts of healings.
3. Working of miracles.

These are the gifts that get things done. i.e. they do something.

Revelation Gifts

1. Word of wisdom.
2. Word of knowledge.
3. Discerning of spirits.

These are the gifts that convey revelation we could not receive in any other way. I.e. they reveal (Make things known).

Vocal Gifts

1. Prophecy.
2. Diverse (Different) kinds of tongues.
3. Interpretation of tongues.

These are the gifts that operate through the human vocal cords. They say something. They are often referred to as the speaking gifts.

Another thing, that is worth knowing about these gifts of the Holy Spirit, is that they are intertwined; meaning, they are like the colours of the rainbow: yellow, red, orange, violet, indigo, blue, green. You may be able to tell the different colours in the rainbow, but may not be able to tell where one ends and another begins. My point is that these *spiritual gifts* often blend into one another. So, you could have the initial *gift of tongues* (Your normal prayer language), that graduates into *diverse (Different) kinds of tongues and interpretation of tongues* kicks in and you know at this point it is prophecy, and the prophecy is coming out as either *a word of knowledge or word of wisdom*.

This is how speaking in tongues opens the door for other spiritual gifts to operate. Paul writes that *"Wherefore let him that speaketh in an unknown tongue pray that he may interpret."* It is clear, here, that we can interpret whatever we speak in tongues (unknown language), we need interpretation because it was not in the language that we readily understood. Paul admonished, *"… desire spiritual gifts, but rather that ye may prophesy."* 1Cor 14:1. If we are able to interpret like Paul said, do you know that this is another gift of the Holy Spirit in operation - Interpretation of tongues.? Remember, tongues plus interpretation of tongues is a prophecy which is another gift of the Holy Spirit, (and if we will follow the example I gave earlier about spiritual gifts being intertwined) the prophecy coming out may be in the form of either word of wisdom or knowledge.

I was, once, in a meeting where a man of God was ministering; a lady gave a word of knowledge. It didn't start with the word of knowledge, but rather, as tongues and then she interpreted what she spoke in tongues. The prophecy was that there were some pregnant women in the meeting that the devil had decided to kill with their pregnancy, they should be called out and prayed for. As the man of God announced it, there were many pregnant women that came out for the prayers. The prophecy came in the language we all understood; but the content of the prophecy, itself, was a word of knowledge in manifestation.

If you desire to flow in the rest of the gifts of the Holy Spirit, what you should do is speak in tongues and make it a usual practice. I remember the first time I prophesied, it was strange, I thought I was just trying to make myself feel good. I didn't realize that prophecy was for edification, exhortation and comfort. I had been praying about my destiny, as usual. I spoke in tongues, suddenly I realized that my normal prayer language changed into another one and I couldn't control or stop it as if I wasn't in charge, I just spoke as the Holy Spirit gave me utterance. After about 5mins, I heard myself say some words that sounded like this, *"I will lift you above your contemporaries, walk before me and be thou perfect"*

I also had another experience, it started with my normal speaking in tongues (prayer language) that ended up as a word of wisdom where I needed direction about a particular thing. I had to make the decision, so I went into the park at night and I prayed in tongues for about an hour. I heard myself say, *"It is a no go area"*. So the following day, I met up with the person that needed my answer and I said I will not be going ahead. These two personal experiences that I have shared are supernatural –what particularly opened the door to me was speaking in tongues.

Speaking In Tongues Refreshes You:

"For with stammering lips and another tongue will he speak to this people. To whom he said, This is the rest wherewith ye may cause the weary to rest; and this is the refreshing: yet they would not hear." Is 28:11-12. This was a prophecy by the prophet Isaiah giving us insight into speaking in tongues. Paul also quoted it in 1Corinthians 14:21, *"In the law it is written, With men of other tongues and other lips will I speak unto this people; and yet for all that will they not hear me, saith the Lord."* Most often, there is a stammering that occurs initially, when you are baptised in the Holy Spirit, that changes over time and becomes or better still sounds like a language. From my experience of praying for people to receive the Holy Spirit with evidence of speaking in tongues, I found it to be like this. Another thing I have noticed is that speaking in tongues refreshes me; it makes me feel ready for the job at hand.

Speaking In Tongues Helps You Wage A Good Warfare:

In writing to the Church at Ephesus, Paul got on the subject of spiritual warfare every child of God faces and also the weapon we have to defeat the enemy. *"Finally, my brethren, be strong in the Lord, and in the power of his might. Put on the whole armour of God, that ye may be able to stand against the wiles of the devil. For we wrestle not against flesh and blood, but against principalities, against powers, against the rulers of the darkness of this world, against spiritual wickedness in high places. Eph 6:10-12.*

Paul said we are not fighting human beings as it were, though the devil uses them, but we are fighting:

1. Principalities
2. Powers
3. Rulers of darkness of this world
4. Spiritual wickedness in high places.

"Wherefore take unto you the whole armour of God, that ye may be able to withstand in the evil day, and having done all, to stand. Stand therefore, having your loins girt about with truth, and having on the breastplate of righteousness; And your feet shod with the preparation of the gospel of peace; Above all, taking the shield of faith, wherewith ye shall be able to quench all the fiery darts of the wicked. And take the helmet of salvation, and the sword of the Spirit, which is the word of God: Praying always with all prayer and supplication in the Spirit, and watching thereunto with all perseverance and supplication for all saints" Eph 6:13-18. Paul went on to show us what to do so as to be able to defeat the enemy. He said we should *"take*

unto you the whole armour of God, that ye may be able to withstand in the evil day, and having done all, to stand" Let's outline the armour of God –

1. Truth.
2. Righteousness.
3. Gospel of peace.
4. Shield of faith.
5. The helmet of salvation.
6. Sword of the Spirit, which is the word of God.
7. Praying always in the Spirit.
8. Watching with all perseverance and supplication for all saints (Interceding for other believers).

One of the armours we are to use against the enemy is that of praying in the Spirit which is not limited to speaking in tongues alone but does include it. Praying in the Spirit, here, is simply praying as led by the Holy Spirit, the one that knows how and what should be prayed. There are times the Holy Spirit gives you prayer points to be prayed in your understanding, in cases like this, you obey and pray as you have been directed, but when you don't have prayer points in your understanding, your best strategy is to speak/pray in tongues.

"When the enemy shall come in like a flood, the Spirit of the LORD shall lift up a standard against him" Isaiah 59:19. This is a prophecy of Prophet Isaiah, which depicts how the Holy Spirit fights for us when the enemy rises against us. The enemy will come against you, but the job of the Holy Spirit is to lift up a standard against the enemy. One of the ways he does that is by giving us utterance, helping us pray in tongues so we can pray the Master's will and thoroughly defeat the enemy. I wrote earlier about the court case I had

to go through, that was a major warfare against my family, ministry and everything concerning me. If I lost, all that I have ever laboured for is gone. My name would have been on the sex offender's list, I would not be able to get a proper job here in the United Kingdom, and above all, if the sentence was more than six months, then I would have to be deported back to Nigeria. I painted this picture so you could see that the victory that the Holy Spirit gave me was a major one. I said earlier that during this time, I prayed much in the Holy Ghost. I will relay to you two experiences, firstly, I had a dream where I called a friend of mine who is a pastor and I told him that there were some individuals behind the court case and that he was to pray for me and the battle will be over. When I woke up, I dialled his number, we spoke and he told me God has answered my prayers and that the battle will soon be over and he prayed for me as I requested.

The second experience happened in the Church. My wife and I went to pray, we waited on the Lord and prayed for about 3 or 4 hours, we spent a large part praying in tongues, but we would both call prayer points as led by the Spirit, at a time I was lost in the Spirit and began to dramatise with my right hand as if I was cancelling something, my tongues at this point also changed. I continued for as long as the Spirit will have me, I didn't stop. My wife stopped to call another prayer, but I told her we should continue. After a while the word of the Lord came to me from Daniel 3:17, *"If it be so, our God whom we serve is able to deliver us from the burning fiery furnace, and he will deliver us out of thine hand, O king"* I printed out a personalised version and pasted it in our room. This is how I personalised it, *"If it be so, our God whom we serve is able to deliver us from the burning fiery fur-*

nace (CASE), and he will deliver us out of thine hand, O king (Crown Prosecuting Service –CPS). True to his word, he delivered me.

WHY IS THE DEVIL ATTACKING THE DOCTRINE OF SPEAKING IN TONGUES?

Looking at all the benefits I have listed above, I will not be exaggerating if I say that speaking in tongues is one of the greatest blessings God gave to the Church Age, and it is just logical to think that the Devil will fight it. The Devil will fight anything that gives believers strength and an upper hand against him. He is ready to go the extra mile to either keep a believer ignorant or deceived.

In general, the apostolic doctrine is a major strength for a believer. That is why one thing that Paul never joked with was the issue of doctrine. The Bible says, *"And they continued stedfastly in the apostles' doctrine…"* Acts 2:42. Doctrine is a teaching, instruction or what is believed. Continuing in the apostles' doctrine – teachings and instructions – is crucial because that is what will establish you and me in the faith.

Paul's Reactions To False Doctrines:

1.   He Places A Curse. *"But though we, or an angel from heaven, preach any other gospel unto you than that which we have preached unto you, let him be accursed. As we said before, so say I now again, if any man preach any other gospel unto you than that ye have received, let him be accursed.* Gal 1:8-9.
2.   He Prepares The Corinthian Church To Be Ready. *"For I am jealous over you with godly jealousy: for I have espoused you to one husband, that I may pres-*

ent you as a chaste virgin to Christ. But I fear, lest by any means, as the serpent beguiled Eve through his subtilty, so your minds should be corrupted from the simplicity that is in Christ. For if he that cometh preacheth another Jesus, whom we have not preached, or if ye receive another spirit, which ye have not received, or another gospel, which ye have not accepted, ye might well bear with him" 2Cor 11:2-4

3. <u>He Told The Ephesian Elders To Be Watchful.</u> "For I know this, that after my departing shall grievous wolves enter in among you, not sparing the flock. Also of your own selves shall men arise, speaking perverse things, to draw away disciples after them. Therefore watch, and remember, that by the space of three years I ceased not to warn every one night and day with tears." Acts 20:29-31.

4. <u>He Delivered Hymenaeus Unto Satan.</u> The reason Paul delivered Hymenaeus to Satan was that of the wrong doctrine. "But shun profane and vain babblings: for they will increase unto more ungodliness. And their word will eat as doth a canker: OF WHOM IS HYMENAEUS AND PHILETUS; WHO CONCERNING THE TRUTH HAVE ERRED, SAYING THAT THE RESURRECTION IS PAST ALREADY; AND OVERTHROW THE FAITH OF SOME" 2Tim 2:16-18. Hymenaeus began to teach wrong doctrines and Paul had no choice, but to hand him over to Satan because according to Paul Hymenaeus' teachings overthrew the faith of some people. He made some people backslide. "Of whom is Hymenaeus and Alexander; whom I have delivered unto Satan, that they may learn not to blaspheme" 1Tim 1:20.

Paul warned Timothy about some activities that will

mark the end of this present Age, amongst others, are the *doctrines of Devils – 1Tim 4:1 (See 1Tim 4:1-6, 2Tim 3:19, 2Tim 4:1-4, Mat 24)*.

DOCTRINES OF DEVILS

In order to overthrow the faith of some people, the Devil has gone the extra mile to concoct his own doctrines – sets of damnable teachings. The question, now, is what are the doctrines of Devil?

1. Any teaching that does not portray Christ as he really is – Lord, Redeemer, Lamb of God, Saviour, God incarnate, Word of God. Or at least portray Him in the light of the scriptures (1John 4:2-3 & 1John 2:22-23).

2. Any teaching that does not show the believer the whole and true picture of God. God is love, but also a judge.

3. Any teaching that does not call a believer into conformity to the image of Christ. Rom 12:1-2; 8:29.

4. Any teaching that makes light of the weightier matter of the kingdom such as repentance, holiness, restitution, prayer and fasting, speaking in tongues, love of God, judgment (Luke 11:42).

5. Any teaching that puts man where God has not placed him. A good example is the practice of the Catholic Church where Mary the mother of Jesus is especially adored and worshipped.

6. Any teaching that puts Celestial beings where God has not placed them. A good example is the worshipping of angels (Col 2:18).

7. Any teaching that does not present marriage as it is in the Bible. The teaching that forbids or makes light of marriage is demonic in origin (1Cor 7).

You can preach or teach a wrong doctrine in two ways, either ignorantly or deliberately.

FEW REASONS WHY THE DEVIL ATTACKS DOCTRINE

Based on my personal findings and authority of God's word, I will give some of the reasons I believe as to why the Devil attacks the Christian doctrine.

1. The Devil knows as long as you are sound in doctrine, you will be sound in obedience. Obedience is the platform of friendship with God.

2. He knows that as long as you imbibe the right doctrines, you will act right. Man's behaviour is a reflection of his belief.

3. As long as you hold on to a proper Bible doctrine, God will be on your side. Balaam could not curse the Israelite until they erred (See Rev 2:14, Num 22 – 31).

4. The Devil knows he can't get you into his side as long as your doctrine is right and you are obedient.

5. As long as your doctrine is right, the Devil knows your safety is guaranteed and of those who hear you. *"Pay close attention to yourself [concentrate on your personal development] and to your teaching; persevere in these things [hold to them], for as you do this you will ensure salvation both for yourself and for those who hear you"* 1Tim 4:16AMP.

6.   The Devil knows that if he can get one man to imbibe a wrong doctrine, that one person can produce millions of people who will adhere to such doctrines of demons. This is the strategy behind strangereligion.

Now, specifically about speaking in tongues, why is the Devil attacking it so much? It is because what tongues offer the believer is numerous. For example, because of speaking in tongues, you and I can, now, talk to God directly, without anyone knowing, including the Devil, as to what I am saying. I am sure he doesn't like that. The Devil also knows that the strength of the believer is somewhat attached to it.

CHAPTER FOUR

DIVERSE KINDS OF TONGUES versus SPEAKING WITH NEW TONGUES.

Someone asked me a question that on the day of Pentecost, people around could hear and understand the tongues that were being said, but nowadays, you don't understand the tongues spoken by many Christians. As sincere or innocent as this question may appear, it is one of the major weapons the Devil is using to make many not desire the precious gift of tongues. Let's look at the incident that happened on the day of Pentecost, "*And when the day of Pentecost was fully come, they were all with one accord in one place. And suddenly there came a sound from heaven as of a rushing mighty wind, and it filled all the house where they were sitting. And there appeared unto them cloven tongues like as of fire, and it sat upon each of them. And they were all filled with the Holy Ghost, and began to speak with other tongues, as the Spirit gave them utterance. And there were dwelling at Jerusalem Jews, devout men, out of every nation under heaven. Now when this was noised abroad, the multitude came together, and were confounded, BECAUSE THAT EVERY MAN HEARD THEM SPEAK IN HIS OWN LANGUAGE. And they were all amazed and marvelled, saying one to another, Behold, are not all these which speak Galilaeans? AND HOW HEAR WE EVERY MAN IN OUR OWN TONGUE, WHEREIN WE WERE BORN? PARTHIANS, AND MEDES, AND ELAMITES, AND THE DWELLERS IN MESOPOTAMIA, AND IN JUDAEA, AND CAPPADOCIA, IN PONTUS, AND ASIA, PHRYGIA,*

AND PAMPHYLIA, IN EGYPT, AND IN THE PARTS OF LIBYA ABOUT CYRENE, AND STRANGERS OF ROME, JEWS AND PROSELYTES, CRETES AND ARABIANS, WE DO HEAR THEM SPEAK IN OUR TONGUES THE WONDERFUL WORKS OF GOD. And they were all amazed, and were in doubt, saying one to another, What meaneth this?* Acts 2:1-12.

EVERY MAN HEARD THEM SPEAK IN HIS OWN LANGUAGE.

Part of what happened on the day of Pentecost as the Holy Spirit came with the evidence of speaking in tongues was that EVERY MAN HEARD THEM SPEAK IN HIS OWN LANGUAGE. One of the vocal gifts of the Holy Spirit known as divers or different kinds of tongues was in operation at the Pentecost, which is different from the prayer language of tongues that is given to all believers at the baptism of the Holy Spirit. Paul wrote concerning this gift that, *"For he that speaketh in an unknown tongue speaketh not unto men, but unto God: FOR NO MAN UNDERSTANDETH HIM; HOWBEIT IN THE SPIRIT HE SPEAKETH MYSTERIES"* 1Cor 14:2. Did you notice Paul said FOR NO MAN UNDERSTANDETH HIM! Because HE IS SPEAKING TO GOD DIRECTLY AND NOT MAN, obviously, what happened at the Pentecost was different because people could hear and understand what was being spoken. The reason for this is that, *"... tongues are for a sign, not to them that believe, but to them that believe not"* 1Cor 14:22. God in His wisdom did that as a sign to the unbelievers around so as to get them inquisitive and eventually be brought to salvation. Because of this, about three thousand souls were won into the kingdom.

Another thing you should observe in this incident

is that those who received the baptism of the Holy Spirit with the evidence of speaking in tongues in the upper room did not understand what they were speaking, but the people who came from the neighbouring villages or town could understand what was being spoken. *"BECAUSE THAT EVERY MAN HEARD THEM SPEAK IN HIS OWN LANGUAGE. And they were all amazed and marvelled, saying one to another, Behold, are not all these which speak Galilaeans? AND HOW HEAR WE EVERY MAN IN OUR OWN TONGUE, WHEREIN WE WERE BORN? PARTHIANS, AND MEDES, AND ELAMITES, AND THE DWELLERS IN MESOPOTAMIA, AND IN JUDAEA, AND CAPPADOCIA, IN PONTUS, AND ASIA, PHRYGIA, AND PAMPHYLIA, IN EGYPT, AND IN THE PARTS OF LIBYA ABOUT CYRENE, AND STRANGERS OF ROME, JEWS AND PROSELYTES, CRETES AND ARABIANS, WE DO HEAR THEM SPEAK IN OUR TONGUES THE WONDERFUL WORKS OF GOD"*

They demonstrated the wonderful works of God, it is not unusual to find this experience as part of the scope of operation of the gift of the Holy Spirit known as divers/different kinds of tongues.

I should also add that there are times you are speaking in tongues, and you don't understand what you are saying, but people around you might understand exactly what you are saying, like the upper room experience. When the gift of diverse kinds of tongues is in operation, the gift of the Holy Spirit known as *interpretation of tongues* may not be needed or be in operation because the people might already understand what was being communicated like the upper room experience.

Jesus, while speaking about the signs that will fol

low a believer, *said that they shall speak with new tongues.* As the Holy Spirit wills, this could be a situation where the speaker is speaking directly to God or he may receive an interpretation of what had been spoken in tongues, which then becomes a prophecy. Speaking in tongues as Paul explained it is the only gift that we are able to express at will (The only gift that is under your control so to speak, at least to a certain level). Remember he said, *I thank my God I speak in tongues more than ye all.* This is because we are the ones that do the speaking, although the Holy Spirit gives us the utterance. However, the Holy Spirit is still in charge because as He wills, he can determine what direction we end up in. What I mean by that is, as the Holy Spirit deems fit, we may end up manifesting any of His gifts.

Few Misconceptions About Speaking In Tongues

Here, I want to discuss the few misconceptions that some people have about speaking in tongues. These are some of the things the Devil is using to hinder people from experiencing the best of God.

Jesus never spoke in tongues, why should I?:

This is one major misconception I, personally, think the Devil is using. Yes, Jesus did not speak in tongues because speaking in tongues is for the Church dispensation. Bible scholars and commentators have divided Bible dispensation into seven categories. Each dispensation is governed by different rules. The word dispensation is from the Greek word *OIKONOMIA* which means, *the management or administration of a household, oversight, administration of a religious economy.* Paul said, "*Now there are diversities of gifts,* but the same Spirit. And there are differences of administra ions, but the same Lord. And there are diversities of operations, but it is the same God which worketh allin all." 1Cor 12:4-6. Did you notice he said there are differences of administration BUT THE SAME LORD, he also said *there are DIVERSITIES OF OPERATIONS, BUT IT IS THE SAME GOD.* That means, things may be done differently (in terms of operations and administrations) but it is the same Lord or God. God told Moses, "*And I appeared unto Abraham, unto Isaac, and unto Jacob, by the name of God Almighty, but by my name JEHOVAH was I not known to them.*" Ex 6:3. Abraham, Isaac and Jacob didn't know that another name of God was JEHOVAH. If you had told them you know they might have argued with you. Paul had an unusual understanding about dispensation. He used it in about five places in scriptures, when he addressed the Church at Ephesus, Corinth and Colossae *(See 1Cor 9:17, Eph 1:10; 2:7; 3:2, Col 1:25).*

It's like Politics, different administrations will adopt different styles, but it is the same Country that is being led. In the United Kingdom, there is the Conservative, Labour, Liberal Democrat, and United Kingdom Independent Parties. All of these have different manifestos, but under one country – England.

Bible Dispensations:

1. Innocence – Gen 1–3
2. Conscience – Gen 3-8
3. Human Government: Gen 9 -11.
4. Promise or Patriarchal: Gen 12 – Ex 19.
5. Law: Ex 20 – Acts 1
6. Grace (This is the Church Age, speaking in tongues is peculiar to this Age): Acts 2 – Rev 20.

7. Millennial Reign of Christ: Rev 20: 4-6.

Different activities were peculiar to these dispensations. Jesus didn't speak in tongues because speaking in tongues is for the Church – The Grace Dispensation/Age. The two gifts of the Holy Spirit that didn't operate in the Old Testament are the gift of speaking in tongues (prayer language)/diverse kinds of tongues and the interpretation of tongues. All these were stored up for the Church era.

Speaking in tongues is for only those in the 5-fold ministry:

There are some who also believe that speaking in tongues is only for those in the 5-fold ministry: Apostles, Prophets, Evangelists, Pastors and Teachers. If you are in any of these offices, the operations of the gifts of the Holy Spirit might differ. However, it is unscriptural to say that the baptism of the Holy Spirit with the evidence of speaking in tongues that Jesus spoke about is only for those in the 5-fold ministry. In Acts 10:44-46, *"While Peter yet spake these words, the Holy Ghost fell on all them which heard the word. And they of the circumcision which believed were astonished, as many as came with Peter, because that on the Gentiles also was poured out the gift of the Holy Ghost. For they heard them speak with tongues, and magnify God..."* The people recorded to be speaking in tongues here are not in the 5-fold ministry. They are gentiles who heard the gospel in the house of Cornelius. This misconception will lead me to my next one.

Also in Acts 8, those who got converted under the Evangelistic ministry of Philip and later spoke in tongues were not in any 5-fold ministry. *"Then Philip went down to the city of Samaria, and preached*

Christ unto ithem. And the people with one accord gave heed unto those things which Philip spake, hearing and seeing the miracles which he did. For unclean spirits, cry-ng with loud voice, came out of many that were possessed with them: and many taken with palsies, and that were lame, were healed. And there was great joy in that city... Now when the apostles which were at Jerusalem heard that Samaria had received the word of God, they sent unto them Peter and John: Who, when they were come down, prayed for them, that they might receive the Holy Ghost: (For as yet he was fallen upon none of them: only they were baptized in the name of the Lord Jesus.) Then laid they their hands on them, and they received the Holy Ghost" Acts 8:5-8 & 14-17. He preached Christ to them, meaning he told them about the salvation plan and the people believed him. Later on, after their water baptism, the apostles came and prayed for the people of Samaria who had believed to receive the Holy Spirit with the evidence of speaking in tongues. They received and spoke in tongues, these were people of Samaria who are not in the 5-fold ministry.

<u>You can only be baptised in the Holy Spirit with the evidence of speaking in tongues only after you have done water baptism:</u>

The level of ignorance in the Church is alarming, even amongst ministers of the gospel. I was in a Church one day and this preacher said something that caught my attention. He said it is fake tongues you are speaking if you are not yet baptised in water. That caught my attention, and immediately scriptures ran through my brain and stopped at the incident that happened in the house of Cornelius. Let's see what happened in the house of Cornelius, as it will benefit you to know a little about who Cornelius was, *"There was a certain man in Caesarea called Cornelius, a centurion of the band called the Italian band, A devout man, and one that feared God with all his house, which gave much alms to the people, and prayed to God always"* Acts 10:1-2 (See Acts 10). God wanted to save him and his household, and in a vision, he was told to contact Peter so that he could experience the salvation plan. Peter got to his house and began to speak. What happened next was that *"While Peter yet spake these words, the Holy Ghost fell on all them which heard the word. And they of the circumcision which believed were astonished, as many as came with Peter, because that on the Gentiles also was poured out the gift of the Holy Ghost. For they heard them speak with tongues, and magnify God"*.

The Holy Spirit fell on them. *How did they know? For they heard them speak with tongues, and magnify God.* Peter was just getting into his sermon, but the Holy Spirit was ready to do His work. We know they were baptised in water after this experience, *"And he commanded them to be baptized in the name of the Lord. Then prayed they him to tarry certain days"* Acts 10:48. After they received the Holy Ghost with evidence of speaking in tongues, Peter commanded that they should be baptised with water. Did you notice that it wasn't the fake Holy Spirit they received because later in the chapter, it was recorded that the household of Cornelius which had received the Holy Ghost as well as we? When Peter was accused of going into the Gentiles, he said to further confirm that what the household of Cornelius received is the same Holy Spirit that fell on them at the Pentecost. *"And as I began to speak,* **the Holy Ghost fell on them, as on us at the beginning**. *Then remembered I the word of* *the Lord, how that he said, John indeed baptized with water; but ye shall be baptized with the Holy Ghost. Forasmuch then as **God gave them the like gift as he did unto us**, who believed on the Lord Jesus Christ; what was I, that I could withstand God?"* Acts 11:15-17. Notice what Peter said THE HOLY GHOST FELL ON THEM, AS ON US AT THE BEGINNING.... GOD GAVE THEM THE LIKE GIFT AS HE DID UNTO US.

In the Kingdom, there is no equation as to how some things must happen. Having said this, the baptism in the Holy Spirit with evidence of speaking in tongues is only for those who believe in Jesus – those who are born again. Once you are born again, you can be baptised in the Holy Spirit immediately and we can, then, schedule your water baptism. Have I said water baptism is irrelevant? No! It is very important, however, you don't have to wait till you have been water baptised before receiving the baptism of the Holy Spirit. Both experiences are important and should be sought; it could come either way as long as you are born again. It is unscriptural seeking either to be baptised in water or in the Holy Spirit without first being born again.

<u>*You can't receive the baptism of the Holy Spirit unless you have someone to minister to you:*</u>

It will be easy to have somebody minister to you, at least you will be a bit confident. However, God in His power has made room for everyone to receive the baptism of the Holy Spirit with the evidence of speaking in tongues in different ways. The first instance of Holy Spirit baptism happened with nobody ministering to those in the Upper Room. What we know is, *"These all continued with one accord in prayer and supplica*

DIVERSE KINDS OF TONGUES versus SPEAKING WITH NEW TONGUES.

tion, with the women, and Mary the mother of Jesus, and with his brethren.... when the day of Pentecost was fully come, they were all with one accord in one place. And suddenly there came a sound from heaven as of a rushing mighty wind, and it filled all the house where they were sitting. And there appeared unto them cloven tongues like as of fire, and it sat upon each of them. And they were all filled with the Holy Ghost, and began to speak with other tongues, as the Spirit gave them utterance." Acts 1:14; 2:1-4. They were in an attitude of prayer, waiting in obedience for the promise of the master and suddenly *there came a sound from heaven as of a rushing mighty wind, and it filled all the house And they were all filled with the Holy Ghost, and began to speak with other tongues, as the Spirit gave them utterance.*

Also, the second time the Apostles experienced the infilling of the Holy Spirit, no one ministered to them. They were in prayers and desperate for an answer. In Acts 2:1-4, they were filled, in Acts 4:31, they were refilled. *"And when they had prayed, the place was shaken where they were assembled together;* **AND THEY WERE ALL FILLED WITH THE HOLY GHOST**, *and they spake the word of God with boldness."* Acts 4:31.

It will be good to have someone to minister to you, but you are not limited to that alone. By prayer and desire, you can receive the baptism in the Holy Spirit with evidence of speaking in tongues. In fact, as you read this book, if you are ready you can receive now. All you need to do is call on the baptiser Himself and He will fill you up. *"I indeed baptize you with water unto repentance: but he that cometh after me is mightier than I, whose shoes I am not worthy to bear:* **he shall baptize you with the Holy Ghost, and with**

***fire*:" Mat 3:11.**

Later on in this book, I will show you based on the authority of God's word, practical steps to take so as to receive the baptism of the Holy Spirit with evidence of speaking in tongues.

<u>*You can only receive the genuine Holy Spirit baptism with the evidence of speaking in tongues if someone standing in the 5-fold ministry ministers to you:*</u>

This may sound strange to you, but there are those who believe this. If you are not in the 5-fold office, they won't allow you minister to them. As much as I do not want to be ministered to by a novice, I can't assume a position that it is until someone standing in the 5-fold office come before I can receive the blessings of Holy Spirit baptism. When Paul received the baptism in the Holy Spirit, we know it was a disciple who laid hands on him. "*And there was a certain <u>disciple</u> at Damascus, named <u>Ananias</u>; and to him said the Lord in a vision, Ananias. And he said, Behold, I am here, Lord. And the Lord said unto him, Arise, and go into the street which is called Straight, and enquire in the house of Judas for one called Saul, of Tarsus: for, behold, he prayeth, And hath seen in a vision a man named Ananias coming in, and putting his hand on him, that he might receive his sight... And Ananias went his way, and entered into the house; and putting his hands on him said, Brother Saul, the Lord, even Jesus, that appeared unto thee in the way as thou camest, hath sent me, that thou mightest receive thy sight, **and be filled with the Holy Ghost**. And immediately there fell from his eyes as it had been scales: and he received sight forthwith, and arose, and was baptized*" Acts 9:10-12 & 17-18.

DIVERSE KINDS OF TONGUES versus SPEAKING WITH NEW TONGUES.

Ananias, who laid hands on Paul, was a sound disciple. He was sound enough to know how to hear God. Do you know that this was the last we read of Ananias, however, Paul later became a mighty Apostle.? I do not prescribe that you allow strange hands to be laid on you. On the other hand, it is not only those in the 5-fold ministry that can minister the baptism of the Holy Spirit with evidence of speaking in tongues. All you need is someone that knows at least to some extent what he is saying and doing. The first time, I ministered the baptism of the Holy Ghost, I was just a young boy in the faith who was assisting a Pastor.

Speaking in tongues ceased with the apostles:

This is erroneous, but there are those who believe this. I came across a study Bible by one of the leading Bible teachers in America. His summation of scriptures that deals with speaking in tongues (either diverse kinds of tongues or interpretation of tongues) were that *it all ceased with the apostles* and whatever anyone in the Charismatic circle may be speaking is gibberish.

Jesus said one of the signs that will follow those who believe in him is that *they shall speak with new tongues*. It is safe to conclude based on what Jesus said that *as long as there are believers (those who believe in Jesus Christ) on the earth, speaking in new tongues will continue. It will always be around.*

Speaking in tongues is not for every believer:

Another widely held misconception about speaking in tongues is that it is not meant for everybody. Someone once said to me speaking in tongues is not my gift. A pastor also told me that God has not given him that gift. Peter wrote, "... *even as our beloved brother Paul also according to the wisdom given unto him hath written unto you; As also in all his epistles, speaking in them of these things; in which are some things hard to be understood, WHICH THEY THAT ARE UNLEARNED AND UNSTABLE WREST, AS THEY DO ALSO THE OTHER SCRIPTURES, UNTO THEIR OWN DESTRUCTION"* 2Peter 3:15-16. This is why Paul told Timothy, *"Study to shew thyself approved unto God, a workman that needeth not to be ashamed, RIGHTLY DIVIDING THE WORD OF TRUTH."* 2Tim 2:15.

The particular misconception we are discussing here is the writing of Paul to the Corinthian Church which has been greatly misunderstood, *"Are all apostles?, are all prophets?, are all teachers?, are all workers of miracles? Have all the gifts of healing? do all speak with tongues? do all interpret?"* 1Cor 12:29-30

To fully understand what Paul was writing, we need to look at 1Cor 12:28 in context. Paul was dealing with public ministry offices (Ministry gifts), he said, *"Now ye are the body of Christ, and members in particular. And God hath set some in the church, first apostles, secondarily prophets, thirdly teachers, after that miracles, then gifts of healings, helps, governments, diversities of tongues"* 1Cor 12:27-28. In his letter to the Ephesian Church he told them, *"And he gave some, apostles; and some, prophets; and some, evangelists; and some, pastors and teachers;"* Eph 4:11. We see clearly from what Paul wrote that God gave some, not all, but some. So, some are Apostles, Prophets, Evangelist, Pastors and Teachers. In communicating this same truth to the believers at Corinth, Paul writes to them: And God hath set some in the church, first apostles, secondarily prophets, thirdly teachers, after that miracles, then gifts of healings, helps, governments, and diversities of tongues. The Church Paul refers to here is not universal, but a general public assembly of believers. He went on to ask them, *"Are all apostles? Are all prophets?, are all teachers? Are all workers of miracles? Have all the gifts of healing?, Do all speak with tongues? Do all interpret?* The answer to the question is no because, "...God gave some.

Firstly, in Corinthians 12:27-30, Paul is not talking about the baptism of the Holy Spirit with evidence of speaking in tongues, rather, he is talking about those with the specific ministry gift given to the Church such as the apostle, prophet, evangelist, teacher, pastor and diversities of tongues is one of such ministry. Do not misconstrue scriptures to make it say what it didn't. In nowhere did Paul say that only a particular set of people can speak in tongues. Instead, he said, *"Wherefore, brethren, covet to prophesy, and forbid not to speak with tongues."* 1Cor 12:39.

CHAPTER FIVE

PRACTICAL STEPS TO RECEIVING THE HOLY SPIRIT.

"Then Peter said unto them, Repent, and be baptized every one of you in the name of Jesus Christ for the remission of sins, and ye shall receive the gift of the Holy Ghost."
Acts 2:38

In this chapter, we will look at some of the practical steps to receiving the Holy Spirit. It is in no particular order, but understanding the whole truth will make it easier for you to minister or receive the baptism in the Holy Spirit, with evidence of speaking with tongues.

Practical Steps:

The Holy Spirit Will Not Speak For You

It is good to know that the Holy Spirit does not speak in tongues, it is the believer that does the speaking. Your spirit does the praying as given utterance or prompted by the Holy Spirit "For if I pray in an unknown tongue, my spirit prayeth, but my understanding is unfruitful. What is it then? I will pray with the spirit, and I will pray with the understanding also: I will sing with the spirit, and I will sing with the understanding also." 1Cor 14:14-15.

From what Paul says here, it is the human spirit that prays in tongues, but the actual words are given or supplied by the Holy Spirit. If you understand this, it will put you in a position to receive the baptism of the Holy Spirit with evidence of speaking in tongues quickly.

You Must Be Hungry & Thirsty:

Jesus said, *"Blessed are they which do hunger and thirst after righteousness: for they shall be filled."* Mat 5:6. He also said, *"In the last day, that great day of the feast, Jesus stood and cried, saying, If any man thirst, let him come unto me, and drink. He that believeth on me, as the scripture hath said, out of his belly shall flow rivers of living water. (But this spake he of the Spirit, which they that believe on him should receive: for the Holy Ghost was not yet given; because that Jesus was not yet glorified.)"* John 7:37-39. To be hungry and thirsty is to be filled! That is a divine rule; wherever God finds a hungry/thirsty soul, He fills such a vessel.

One of the easiest experiences I have had in praying for people to receive the baptism of the Holy Spirit with evidence of speaking in tongues, was when I served as an assistant pastor. A brother came to me looking very desperate, he said he wanted to be baptised in the Holy Spirit and that I should pray for him, I told him if he is ready, God – the baptizer – is ready. And I said, "receive it now", it was like a switch, he exploded speaking fluently.

The reason I love to teach and explain things, especially when it comes to the subject of Holy Spirit baptism is because once the understanding is enlightened and hunger/thirst for this spiritual blessing is stirred up, it doesn't take long to receive.

(As you are reading, if you believe and you are

hungry, receive ye the Holy Spirit now in Jesus' name).

Remember, *If any man thirst, let him come unto me, and drink. He that believeth on me, as the scripture hath said, out of his belly shall flow rivers of living water. (But this spake he of the Spirit, which they that believe on him should receive.*

The Holy Spirit Belongs To You:

On the day of Pentecost, Peter said, "*...unto them, Repent, and be baptized every one of you in the name of Jesus Christ for the remission of sins, and ye shall receive the gift of the Holy Ghost. For the promise is unto you, and to your children, and to all that are afar off, even as many as the LORD our God shall call.*" Acts 2:38-39. Did you notice it says the promise is unto you and to your children, and to all that are afar off, even as many as the Lord our God shall call. That means the Holy Spirit is for all. He belongs to you and me.

It will do something different to you when you know that a particular thing is yours. Your level of boldness will surely increase. So it is when you know that the Holy Spirit belongs to you, it will help you maximize His ministry. Jesus said, "*And I will pray the Father, and he shall give you another Comforter, that he may abide with you for ever; Even the Spirit of truth; whom the world cannot receive, because it seeth him not, neither knoweth him: but ye know him; for he dwelleth with you, and shall be in you. I will not leave you comfortless: I will come to you... But the Comforter, which is the Holy Ghost, whom the Father will send in my name, he shall teach you all things, and bring all things to your remembrance, whatsoever I have said unto you.*" John 14:16-18, 26.

The promise of the Father is the Holy Spirit and one of the things he has come to do is to indwell the believer, fill the believer up and also give him utterance to speak in new tongues. As Peter said, the prerequisite to receiving Him is to repent. *"Then Peter said unto them, Repent, and be baptized every one of you in the name of Jesus Christ for the remission of sins, and ye shall receive the gift of the Holy Ghost."* Acts 2:38

Be Bold And Don't Give Room To Fear:

Whenever I minister the baptism of the Holy Spirit, one thing I say all the time is for the candidates never to be afraid. I also bind the spirit of fear. There are those who are afraid of all manner of things. Some are not bold because they think *how can I be speaking a language I don't understand*. Some think what if I *get the wrong spirit*.

This is one of the reasons why it is good to teach correctly so that the candidate can get rid of any wrong doctrine, or prejudices about speaking in tongues. Some people's problem is their mind, if you get it renewed, you will get results. Paul told Timothy, *"For God hath not given us the spirit of fear; but of power, and of love, and of a sound mind."* 2Tim 1:7.

When We Ask For The Holy Spirit We Receive Him:

It is also a good practice to let the candidate know that when we ask for the Holy Spirit, God gives what we ask for and what we have to do is receive. Jesus said, *"And I say unto you, Ask, and it shall be given you; seek, and ye shall find; knock, and it shall be opened unto you. For every one that asketh receiveth; and he that seeketh findeth, and to him that knocketh it shall* be opened. *If a son shall ask bread of any of you that s a father, will he give him a stone?, or if he ask a fish, will he for a fish give him a serpent?, Or if he shall ask an egg, will he offer him a scorpion?, If ye then, being evil, know how to give good gifts unto your children: How Much More Shall Your Heavenly Father Give The Holy Spirit To Them That Ask Him?"*, Luke 11:9-13. As a father, I want the best for and give the best to my children. Jesus said, God does much more for his children. In, as much as, no earthly father will give poison to his son when he asks for fish, so when you ask for the Holy Spirit, what you should expect is the Holy Spirit.

Speak By Faith:

My final instruction is often *"Now begin to speak in tongues by faith"*. Everything in the kingdom is by faith, the just shall live by faith - this is what the Bible says. Speaking in tongues is an act of faith.

After I pray for the candidate/s, I say to them, now do not speak any language you knew before, the Holy Spirit will give you the words (utterance), but you have to speak it out. I continue by saying what *Jesus said out of your belly shall flow rivers of living water*. And I say, there is a bubbling in your belly, the words are given to you now, open your mouth and speak. You don't have to understand, speak in Jesus' name.

God is faithful, he backs up His words.

Hands Might Be Laid On You:

From my personal experience, there are those who might need hands to be laid on before such would receive the gift of the Holy Spirit. I lay hands when I see that a candidate is struggling a bit to receive. There is the doctrine of *laying on of hands* (See Heb 6:1-3). There are also some people who are specially gifted and to lay hands and minister the baptism of the Holy Spirit, which will always be accompanied with speaking in tongues.

In Acts 8, we saw the ministry of Philip in the city of Samaria. It was recorded that they believed the gospel and were baptised in water. This seems to be how far Philip could bring them, something else, however, happened when the apostle came. *"Now when the apostles which were at Jerusalem heard that Samaria had received the word of God, they sent unto them Peter and John: Who, when they were come down, prayed for them, that they might receive the Holy Ghost: (For as yet he was fallen upon none of them: only they were baptized in the name of the Lord Jesus.) Then laid they their hands on them, and they received the Holy Ghost"* Acts 8:14-17.

When Peter and John arrived, they operated in the somewhat higher power of the Holy Spirit as we see what began to happen when they arrived. They – Peter and John – prayed for the people of Samaria to receive the Holy Spirit and then laid hands on them. If you read further, Bible says, *"And WHEN SIMON SAW THAT THROUGH LAYING ON OF THE APOSTLES' HANDS THE HOLY GHOST WAS GIVEN, he offered them money"* V18. The Holy Spirit was given through the laying on of the apostles' hands.

Kenneth E. Hagin of blessed memory also said that the Lord gave him this type of ministry where *the Holy Spirit will be given – received by the candidates – when he lays hands on them with the evidence of speaking in tongues.*

It is a good thing to let those seeking to be filled with the Holy Spirit, know that hands might be laid on them so as to receive Him.

Take Authority Over Lying Spirit:

It is very well possible that a lying spirit might hinder an individual from receiving the Holy Spirit. If this is discerned, or as a precautionary measure, you should bind that spirit and then explain to the candidate not to allow any lying spirit deceive him/her into believing that the utterance by the Holy Spirit which they are to speak out is rubbish.

It is also helpful to point out to the candidate that he/she might not be as fluent as the Pastor or the one ministering the baptism of the Holy Ghost.

CHAPTER SIX

A BETTER WAY TO PRAY

"But God hath revealed them unto us by his Spirit: for the Spirit searcheth all things, yea, the deep things of God. For what man knoweth the things of a man, save the spirit of man which is in him? Even so the things of God knoweth no man, but the Spirit of God. Now we have received, not the spirit of the world, but the spirit which is of God; that we might know the things that are freely given to us of God."
1Cor 2:10-12.

There are different ministries that the Holy Spirit has for a believer, one of which is to help in the place of prayer. The Holy Spirit supplies help that nothing else can. It is, therefore, wisdom to settle down and know exactly what and how the Holy Spirit operates His ministry towards the believer.

There is a depth in prayer that you and I can't reach without the help of the Holy Spirit.

MINISTRY OF REVELATION

One of the ministries of the Holy Spirit is the ministry of revelation. The Holy Spirit brings revelation to us so that we know what we should know and go about it in a proper way. Without revelation, the believer will be in the dark and deception which is where the Devil loves to operate. If you have no revelation of the Spirit, you will suffer a loss in one way or the other.

Paul said, *"But God hath revealed them unto us by his Spirit: for the Spirit searcheth all things, yea, the deep things of God..."*

Did you notice that phrase *"God hath revealed them unto us by his Spirit"* The word revealed here means to uncover, lay open what has been veiled or covered up, disclose, make known, make manifest and take off the cover. This means many things are covered up, which is not visible neither accessible by or to the human natural sense, but can only be accessed by the Holy Spirit.

When you engage the Holy Spirit in the place of prayer, one thing you will enjoy is His revelational ministry. He will uncover what has been covered. He may uncover to you the next step to take in your life, he may uncover to you why things are not going well.

On several occasions whilst I minister in the Church or I am doing my personal prayers, the Holy Spirit brings revelation of different sorts. I remember a time I had an invitation to minister at a particular Church, I spoke to a few people I respected if I should go. One said I should go and another said I should go and pray, so I went to pray and as I was praying, the word of the Lord came to me – A revelation of the word by the ministry of the Spirit – and said, *"They have Moses and the Prophets, if they don't hear them, they will not hear you"*. So I called the person that invited me and told him that God said you have Moses and the Prophets, you don't need me.

In the Scriptures, we see both in the Old Testa

ment and the New Testament where, when some individuals were praying, the Holy Spirit brought revelation – insight – about what to do, so as to have victory. One major way to secure victory in the spirit is to follow and obey the revelation the Holy Spirit brings along.

Old Testament

The first example I want to refer to, where the Holy Spirit brought a revelation as a result of prayer or seeking the face of God was when the enemy came against Jehoshaphat, king of Judah. *"And Jehoshaphat feared, and set himself to seek the LORD, and proclaimed a fast throughout all Judah. And Judah gathered themselves together, to ask help of the LORD: even out of all the cities of Judah they came to seek the LORD"* 2CHRON 20:3-4. The king declared a national fast and sought the face of God, whilst they were praying there was a revelation by the Holy Spirit. *"Then upon Jahaziel the son of Zechariah, the son of Benaiah, the son of Jeiel, the son of Mattaniah, a Levite of the sons of Asaph, came the Spirit of the LORD in the midst of the congregation; And he said, Hearken ye, all Judah, and ye inhabitants of Jerusalem, and thou king Jehoshaphat, Thus saith the LORD unto you, Be not afraid nor dismayed by reason of this great multitude; for the battle is not yours, but God's. To morrow go ye down against them: behold, they come up by the cliff of Ziz; and ye shall find them at the end of the brook, before the wilderness of Jeruel. Ye shall not need to fight in this battle: set yourselves, stand ye still, and see the salvation of the LORD with you, O Judah and Jerusalem: fear not, nor be dismayed; to morrow go out against them: for the LORD will be with you."* 2Chron 20:14-17.

The revelation that the Holy Spirit brought was both instructive and prophetic. God told them what they had to do and also the outcome of the battle.

The Spirit came upon Jahaziel and gave the following prophetic instructions.

1. Be not afraid because of the numbers of the enemies coming against you.
2. The battle is not yours. God takes up their battle officially so to speak.
3. They were to go out the next day, not stay indoors.
4. They also knew the place where the enemy was coming from.
5. Be ready for the enemy, and also be ready for what the Lord will do.

There were no other ways they could have known this if the Spirit of God did not bring forth a revelation.

New Testament

One major mark of the earthly ministry of Jesus was that he prayed very much and so, he had a revelation about many things and particularly he also moved in the gift of the Holy Spirit (See John 1:47-50; 5:6 & Luke 13:11-16). One incident stood out, though the Bible didn't say specifically that the Holy Spirit brought a revelation, but we can conclude that it was the Holy Spirit.

Jesus said to Peter, "...*Simon, Simon, behold, Satan hath desired to have you, that he may sift you as wheat. But I have prayed for thee, that thy faith fail not: and when thou art converted, strengthen thy brethren*" Luke 22:31-32.

The Holy Spirit gave a revelation –an insight – into the plan of the enemy for Peter. I believe that Jesus must have received this revelation in the place of prayer because he did say *I HAVE PRAYED FOR THEE*. Without the Holy Spirit bringing revelation about situations, events and circumstances, the enemy will take advantage of us and have the upper hand. You must be spirit led and a prayer addict if you need to enjoy more revelation through the ministry of the Holy Spirit.

THE HOLY SPIRIT MINISTERS LIFE

In John 11, we have the story of Lazarus, who was sick and later died. The end result was that Jesus raised him from the dead. What I want to draw your attention to, is, to see another ministry of the Holy Spirit which is to give life. Paul said, *"But if the Spirit of him that raised up Jesus from the dead dwell in you, he that raised up Christ from the dead SHALL ALSO QUICKEN YOUR MORTAL BODIES BY HIS SPIRIT THAT DWELLETH IN YOU."* Rom 8:11

Jesus also said, *"IT IS THE SPIRIT THAT QUICKENETH; the flesh profiteth nothing: the words that I speak unto you, they are spirit, and they are life"* John 6:63. The word quickeneth from the two passages means to make alive or revitalise.

Jesus knew that Lazarus was going to die and after he died, he stood back four days. *"JESUS THEREFORE AGAIN GROANING IN HIMSELF COMETH TO THE GRAVE. IT WAS A CAVE, AND A STONE LAY UPON IT… Then they took away the stone from the place where the dead was laid. And Jesus lifted up his eyes, and said, Father, I thank thee that thou hast heard me. And I knew that thou hearest me always: but because of the people which stand by I said it, that they may believe that thou hast sent me. And when he thus had spoken, he cried with a loud voice, Lazarus, come forth And he that was dead came forth, bound hand and foot with graveclothes: and his face was bound about with a napkin. Jesus saith unto them, Loose him, and let him go."* John 11:38 & 41-44.

It is evident that the Devil killed Lazarus untimely, by first introducing sickness and later, death. Jesus, on the other hand, came to give life and he did that by the ministry of the Spirit through prayer because we read that Jesus therefore again GROANING in himself cometh to the grave. The word groaning is what we usually see when an individual is in the place of prayer and the Holy Spirit helps them bring those words out. Paul refers to them as, *"Likewise the Spirit also helpeth our infirmities: for we know not what we should pray for as we ought: BUT THE SPIRIT ITSELF MAKETH INTERCESSION FOR US WITH GROANINGS WHICH CANNOT BE UTTERED"* Rom 8:26.

It wasn't God who killed Lazarus, but the Devil. If it was God, Jesus wouldn't be seeking to raise him up as that will be working opposite his father, rather, we know that Jesus said the Devil came to steal, kill and destroy, but he came to give life. The Holy Spirit makes alive, whatever is dead or dying in the life of any believer.

I am persuaded that there are things in your life that may die prematurely if you do not bring upon yourself the ministry of life of the Holy Spirit through prayers. The prayers – groaning – Jesus did in himself brought back Lazarus to life. If things that are dead in your life must be brought back to life you must learn to let *THE SPIRIT HIMSELF MAKE INTERCESSION FOR US (YOU) WITH GROANINGS WHICH CANNOT BE UTTERED.*

This is where praying in tongues comes in. When we pray in tongues as helped by the Holy Spirit, in many cases, we are groaning and thereby, birthing out the will of the father on the earth.

To remain unstoppable by the enemy, you must allow the Holy Spirit to take your prayer life to the next level, by constantly and consistently yielding to Him. Paul said, *"Praying always with all prayer and supplication in the Spirit, and watching thereunto with all perseverance and supplication for all saints"* Eph 6:18. You know that you can't pray adequately, correctly and accurately for all saints without allowing the Holy Spirit to dictate to you what and how you will pray. Some of these prayers will be prayed in your known language, but it will be with the help of the Spirit. Did you also notice that Paul said *PRAYING ALWAYS WITH ALL PRAYERS AND SUPPLICATION IN THE SPIRIT!* What that is saying is that the only way to pray and become fruitful – see results of prayers – is to pray always in the Spirit. Not once in a while and not when you feel like it, *BUT ALWAYS.*

Let me close this chapter with the words of Paul *PRAYING ALWAYS WITH ALL PRAYERS AND SUPPLICATION IN THE SPIRIT!*

(For further insight about the ministry of the Holy Spirit, get my book PARAKLETOS).

This is where praying in tongues comes in. When we pray in tongues as helped by the Holy Spirit, in many cases, we are groaning and thereby, birthing out the will of the father on the earth.

PRAYER FOR SALVATION

Except a man is born again he will never and can never see the kingdom of God. Salvation is mandatory for anyone that desires to enter into the kingdom of God. Without salvation, no man will see God. You need to be saved from the wrath of God that is coming upon this disobedient generation. Please pray like this . . . . . .

Heavenly Father, I come to You in the name of Your Son Jesus. Your word says that "And it shall come to pass, that whosoever shall call on the name of the Lord be saved". Act 2:21. I am calling on you now. I pray and desire that you come into my heart now and be my Lord and Saviour according to your word which says, "That if thou shalt confess with thy mouth the Lord Jesus, and shalt believe in thine heart that God hath raised him from the dead, thou shalt be saved. For with the heart man believeth unto righteousness, and with the mouth confession is made unto salvation". Romans 10:9-10. I do that now, I believe in my heart that Jesus Christ died for me and was raised from the dead on the third day. I confess with my mouth that he is Lord. I ask that you forgive me of my sins and cleanse me with your blood. This I ask for in Jesus name. Amen

We believe you have been saved. Look for a Bible believing and teaching church that will enhance your growth in the knowledge and grace of God.

PRAYER FOR THE BAPTISM IN THE HOLY GHOST

Power is needed to run the race which you have just begun. Jesus Christ told His disciples never to go out and do anything until they have been endued with power. The power is made available by the baptism of the Holy Spirit with an evidence of speaking in tongues. God desires that you should be baptized and speak in the heavenly language. The Holy Spirit will give you the utterance, but you will have to open your mouth and speak out boldly. You do not have to understand what the words mean just say it out as you receive it. Please pray like this:

Father Lord, I come to you in the name of Jesus Christ and I ask you to fill me with the Holy Spirit now with the evidence of speaking with tongues, because you said in your word that, " . . . If ye then, being evil, know how to give good gifts unto your children: how much more shall your heavenly Father give the Holy Spirit to them that ask him . . . .". Luke 11:13. I also know from your word that, ". . . everyone who asks receives, and he who seeks finds, and to him who knocks it will be opened . . . " Mathew 7:8NKJV. Holy Spirit rise up within me now as I begin to praise God. I am ready and fully expect to speak in tongues now as You give me utterance in the name of Jesus Christ. Amen.

Now lift up your hands and begin to praise God, then speak those words as they come to you now in Jesus' name. Amen!

Having received the baptism of the Holy Ghost with the evidence of speaking in tongues you must constantly speak in your prayer language.

ABOUT THE BOOK

And these signs shall follow them that believe; In my name shall they cast out devils; they shall speak with new tongues; They shall take up serpents; and if they drink any deadly thing, it shall not hurt them; they shall lay hands on the sick, and they shall recover" Mark 16:14-18

Jesus, whilst rounding up his earthly ministry, gave the Apostles a great task which is commonly called "The Great Commission". He moved on from that and said that there were some signs that would follow anyone who believes in Him. Apart from the fact that anyone who believes in Jesus would be saved and not be damned, there were other things that would begin to follow such persons.

These were the signs Jesus said would follow such individual –

1. They will cast out devils (Demons or unclean spirit) in Jesus' name.
2. They will speak with new tongues. (They will receive a prayer language)
3. They will be able to take up serpents. (This is divine immunity against Satanic attacks, for we know that the devil is called serpent, that old dragon – Rev 20:2)
4. Peradventure they drink any deadly thing, they will not be hurt. (This is also divine immunity).
5. They will lay hands on the sick, and the sick person will recover. (This is a supernatural ability against sickness, to bring wholeness and wellness into anyone sick)

This book is about power for a dynamic prayer life be

cause the other signs might not be fully experienced if the prayer life of the believer is not sound and dynamic.

This book reveals why every believer should speak with tongues and the benefits. It also clarifies some misconceptions about the subject of speaking with tongues.

ABOUT THE AUTHOR

Ayodeji D. Olusanmi is a teacher and a preacher of the gospel. A dynamic pastor of a branch of Mountain of Fire and Miracle Ministries – United Kingdom. He studied in the UK as a Biomedical Scientist. He is the author of *The Prayer that Works, The Testimony of a Youth, Parakletos, Godly Wisdom for Success at the Workplace, Nothing Shall By Any Means Hurt You, Lessons from My Father*. He is married to Margaret and they are blessed with children.

www.ingramcontent.com/pod-product-compliance
Lightning Source LLC
LaVergne TN
LVHW011735060526
838200LV00051B/3173